Employers are responsible for providing a safe and healthy workplace for their employees. OSHA's role is to promote the safety and health of America's working men and women by setting and enforcing standards; providing training, outreach and education; establishing partnerships; and encouraging continual improvement in workplace safety and health.

This informational booklet provides a general overview of a particular topic related to OSHA standards. It does not alter or determine compliance responsibilities in OSHA standards or the *Occupational Safety and Health Act of 1970*. Because interpretations and enforcement policy may change over time, you should consult current OSHA administrative interpretations and decisions by the Occupational Safety and Health Review Commission and the courts for additional guidance on OSHA compliance requirements.

This publication is in the public domain and may be reproduced, fully or partially, without permission. Source credit is requested but not required.

This information is available to sensory impaired individuals upon request. Voice phone: (202) 693-1999; teletypewriter (TTY) number: (877) 889-5627.

Permit-Required Confined Spaces

U.S. Department of Labor

Occupational Safety and Health Administration

OSHA 3138-01R
2004

Contents

Introduction

Many workplaces contain spaces that are considered to be "confined" because their configurations hinder the activities of employees who must enter into, work in or exit from them. In many instances, employees who work in confined spaces also face increased risk of exposure to serious physical injury from hazards such as entrapment, engulfment and hazardous atmospheric conditions. Confinement itself may pose entrapment hazards and work in confined spaces may keep employees closer to hazards such as machinery components than they would be otherwise. For example, confinement, limited access and restricted airflow can result in hazardous conditions that would not normally arise in an open workplace.

The terms "permit-required confined space" and "permit space" refer to spaces that meet OSHA's definition of a "confined space" and contain health or safety hazards. For this reason, OSHA requires workers to have a permit to enter these spaces. Throughout this publication, the term "permit space" will be used to describe a "permit-required confined space."

Definitions

By definition, a **confined space**:

- Is large enough for an employee to enter fully and perform assigned work;
- Is not designed for continuous occupancy by the employee; and
- Has a limited or restricted means of entry or exit.

These spaces may include underground vaults, tanks, storage bins, pits and diked areas, vessels, silos and other similar areas.

By definition, a **permit-required confined space** has one or more of these characteristics:

- Contains or has the potential to contain a hazardous atmosphere;
- Contains a material with the potential to engulf someone who enters the space;
- Has an internal configuration that might cause an entrant to be trapped or asphyxiated by inwardly converging walls or by a

floor that slopes downward and tapers to a smaller cross section; and/or

- Contains any other recognized serious safety or health hazards.

OSHA's Confined Space Standard

OSHA's standard for confined spaces (29 CFR 1910.146) contains the requirements for practices and procedures to protect employ-ees in general industry from the hazards of entering permit spaces.

Employers in general industry must evaluate their workplaces to determine if spaces are permit spaces. (See flow chart, page 5.) If a workplace contains permit spaces, the employer must inform exposed employees of their existence, location and the hazards they pose. This can be done by posting danger signs such as "DANGER—PERMIT-REQUIRED CONFINED SPACE—AUTHORIZED ENTRANTS ONLY" or using an equally effective means.

If employees are not to enter and work in permit spaces, employers must take effective measures to prevent them from entering these spaces. If employees are expected to enter permit spaces, the employer must develop a written permit space program and make it available to employees or their representatives.

Alternative to a full permit entry

Under certain conditions described in the standard, the employer may use alternate procedures for worker entry into a permit space. For example, if an employer can demonstrate with monitoring and inspection data that the only hazard is an actual or potential hazardous atmosphere that can be made safe for entry using continuous forced air ventilation, the employer may be exempted from some requirements, such as permits and attendants. However, even in these circumstances, the employer must test the internal atmosphere of the space for oxygen content, flammable gases and vapors, and the potential for toxic air contaminants before any employee enters it. The employer must also provide continuous ventilation and verify that the required measurements are performed before entry.

Permit-Required Confined Space Decision Flow Chart

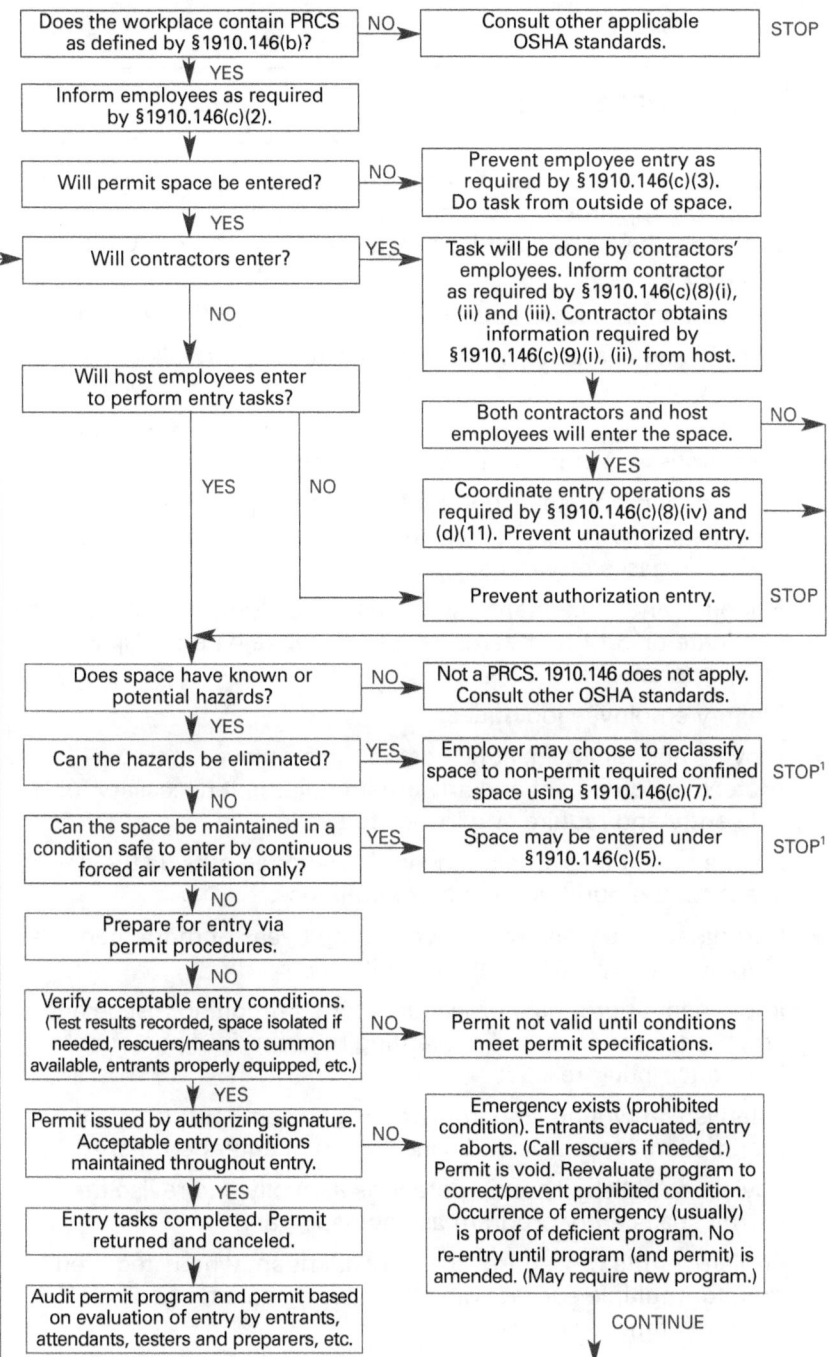

[1] Spaces may have to be evacuated and reevaluated if hazards arise during entry.

Source: 29 CFR 1910.146 Appendix A.

Written Programs

Any employer who allows employee entry into a permit space must develop and implement a written program for the space. Among other things, the OSHA standard requires the employer's written program to:

- Implement necessary measures to prevent unauthorized entry;
- Identify and evaluate permit space hazards before allowing employee entry;
- Test atmospheric conditions in the permit space before entry operations and monitor the space during entry;
- Perform appropriate testing for the following atmospheric hazards in this sequence: oxygen, combustible gases or vapors, and toxic gases or vapors;
- Establish and implement the means, procedures and practices to eliminate or control hazards necessary for safe permit space entry operations;
- Identify employee job duties;
- Provide and maintain, at no cost to the employee, personal protective equipment and any other equipment necessary for safe entry and require employees to use it;
- Ensure that at least one attendant is stationed outside the permit space for the duration of entry operations;
- Coordinate entry operations when employees of more than one employer are working in the permit space;
- Implement appropriate procedures for summoning rescue and emergency services, and preventing unauthorized personnel from attempting rescue;
- Establish, in writing, and implement a system for the preparation, issue, use and cancellation of entry permits;
- Review established entry operations annually and revise the permit space entry program as necessary; and
- Implement the procedures that any attendant who is required to monitor multiple spaces will follow during an emergency in one or more of those spaces.

Controlling Hazards

The employer's written program should establish the means, procedures and practices to eliminate or control hazards necessary for safe permit space entry operations. These may include:

- Specifying acceptable entry conditions;
- Isolating the permit space;
- Providing barriers;
- Verifying acceptable entry conditions; and
- Purging, making inert, flushing or ventilating the permit space.

Equipment for safe entry

In addition to personal protective equipment, other equipment that employees may require for safe entry into a permit space includes:

- Testing, monitoring, ventilating, communications and lighting equipment;
- Barriers and shields;
- Ladders; and
- Retrieval devices.

Detection of hazardous conditions

If hazardous conditions are detected during entry, employees must immediately leave the space. The employer must evaluate the space to determine the cause of the hazardous atmosphere and modify the program as necessary.

When entry to permit spaces is prohibited, the employer must take effective measures to prevent unauthorized entry. Non-permit confined spaces must be evaluated when changes occur in their use or configuration and, where appropriate, must be reclassified as permit spaces.

A space with no potential to have atmospheric hazards may be classified as a non-permit confined space only when all hazards are eliminated in accordance with the standard. If entry is required to eliminate hazards and obtain data, the employer must follow specific procedures in the standard.

Informing Contract Employees

Employers must inform any contractors whom they hire to enter permit spaces about:

- The permit spaces and permit space entry requirements;
- Any identified hazards;
- The employer's experience with the space, such as knowledge of hazardous conditions; and
- Precautions or procedures to be followed when in or near permit spaces.

When employees of more than one employer are conducting entry operations, the affected employers must coordinate entry operations to ensure that affected employees are appropriately protected from permit space hazards. The employer also must give contractors any other pertinent information regarding hazards and operations in permit spaces and be debriefed at the conclusion of entry operations.

Entry Permits

A permit, signed by the entry supervisor, must be posted at all entrances or otherwise made available to entrants before they enter a permit space. The permit must verify that pre-entry preparations outlined in the standard have been completed. The duration of entry permits must not exceed the time required to complete an assignment.

Entry permits must include:

- Name of permit space to be entered, authorized entrant(s), eligible attendants and individuals authorized to be entry supervisors;
- Test results;
- Tester's initials or signature;
- Name and signature of supervisor who authorizes entry;
- Purpose of entry and known space hazards;
- Measures to be taken to isolate permit spaces and to eliminate or control space hazards;

- Name and telephone numbers of rescue and emergency services and means to be used to contact them;
- Date and authorized duration of entry;
- Acceptable entry conditions;
- Communication procedures and equipment to maintain contact during entry;
- Additional permits, such as for hot work, that have been issued authorizing work in the permit space;
- Special equipment and procedures, including personal protective equipment and alarm systems; and
- Any other information needed to ensure employee safety.

Cancelled entry permits

The entry supervisor must cancel entry permits when an assignment is completed or when new conditions exist. New conditions must be noted on the canceled permit and used in revising the permit space program. The standard requires that the employer keep all canceled entry permits for at least one year.

Worker Training

Before the initial work assignment begins, the employer must provide proper training for all workers who are required to work in permit spaces. After the training, employers must ensure that the employees have acquired the understanding, knowledge and skills necessary to safely perform their duties. Additional training is required when:

- The job duties change;
- A change occurs in the permit space program or the permit space operation presents any new hazard; and
- An employee's job performance shows deficiencies.

In addition to this training, rescue team members also require training in CPR and first aid. Employers must certify that this training has been provided.

After completion of training, the employer must keep a record of employee training and make it available for inspection by employees

and their authorized representatives. The record must include the employee's name, the trainer's signature or initials and dates of the training.

Assigned Duties

Authorized entrant

Authorized entrants are required to:

- Know space hazards, including information on the means of exposure such as inhalation or dermal absorption, signs of symptoms and consequences of the exposure;
- Use appropriate personal protective equipment properly;
- Maintain communication with attendants as necessary to enable them to monitor the entrant's status and alert the entrant to evacuate when necessary;
- Exit from the permit space as soon as possible when:
  - Ordered by the authorized person;
  - He or she recognizes the warning signs or symptoms of exposure;
  - A prohibited condition exists; or
  - An automatic alarm is activated.
- Alert the attendant when a prohibited condition exists or when warning signs or symptoms of exposure exist.

Attendant

The attendant is required to:

- Remain outside the permit space during entry operations unless relieved by another authorized attendant;
- Perform non-entry rescues when specified by the employer's rescue procedure;
- Know existing and potential hazards, including information on the mode of exposure, signs or symptoms, consequences and physiological effects;

- Maintain communication with and keep an accurate account of those workers entering the permit space;
- Order evacuation of the permit space when:
  - A prohibited condition exists;
  - A worker shows signs of physiological effects of hazard exposure;
  - An emergency outside the confined space exists; and
  - The attendant cannot effectively and safely perform required duties.
- Summon rescue and other services during an emergency;
- Ensure that unauthorized people stay away from permit spaces or exit immediately if they have entered the permit space;
- Inform authorized entrants and the entry supervisor if any unauthorized person enters the permit space; and
- Perform no other duties that interfere with the attendant's primary duties.

Entry supervisor

Entry supervisors are required to:

- Know space hazards including information on the mode of exposure, signs or symptoms and consequences;
- Verify emergency plans and specified entry conditions such as permits, tests, procedures and equipment before allowing entry;
- Terminate entry and cancel permits when entry operations are completed or if a new condition exists;
- Verify that rescue services are available and that the means for summoning them are operable;
- Take appropriate measures to remove unauthorized entrants; and
- Ensure that entry operations remain consistent with the entry permit and that acceptable entry conditions are maintained.

Emergencies

Rescue service personnel

The standard requires employers to ensure that responders are capable of responding to an emergency in a timely manner. Employers must provide rescue service personnel with personal protective and rescue equipment, including respirators, and training in how to use it. Rescue service personnel also must receive the authorized entrants training and be trained to perform assigned rescue duties.

The standard also requires that all rescuers be trained in first aid and CPR. At a minimum, one rescue team member must be currently certified in first aid and CPR. Employers must ensure that practice rescue exercises are performed yearly and that rescue services are provided access to permit spaces so they can practice rescue operations. Rescuers also must be informed of the hazards of the permit space.

Harnesses and retrieval lines

Authorized entrants who enter a permit space must wear a chest or full body harness with a retrieval line attached to the center of their backs near shoulder level or above their heads. Wristlets may be used if the employer can demonstrate that the use of a chest or full body harness is not feasible or creates a greater hazard.

Also, the employer must ensure that the other end of the retrieval line is attached to a mechanical device or a fixed point outside the permit space. A mechanical device must be available to retrieve someone from vertical type permit spaces more than five feet (1.524 meters) deep.

MSDS

If an injured entrant is exposed to a substance for which a Material Safety Data Sheet (MSDS) or other similar written information is required to be kept at the worksite, that MSDS or other written information must be made available to the medical facility personnel treating the exposed entrant.

OSHA Assistance

OSHA can provide extensive help through a variety of programs, including technical assistance about effective safety and health programs, state plans, workplace consultations, voluntary protection programs, strategic partnerships, training and education, and more. An overall commitment to workplace safety and health can add value to your business, to your workplace, and to your life.

Safety and Health Program Management Guidelines

Effective management of employee safety and health protection is a decisive factor in reducing the extent and severity of work-related injuries and illnesses and their related costs. In fact, an effective safety and health program forms the basis of good employee protection and can save time and money and increase productivity and reduce employee injuries, illnesses, and related workers' compensation costs.

To assist employers and employees in developing effective safety and health programs, OSHA published recommended Safety and Health Program Management Guidelines (54 Federal Register (16): 3904-3916, January 26, 1989). These voluntary guidelines can be applied to all places of employment covered by OSHA.

The guidelines identify four general elements critical to the development of a successful safety and health management system:

- Management leadership and employee involvement,
- Worksite analysis,
- Hazard prevention and control, and
- Safety and health training.

The guidelines recommend specific actions, under each of these general elements, to achieve an effective safety and health program. The *Federal Register* notice is available online at www.osha.gov.

State Programs

The *Occupational Safety and Health Act of 1970* (OSH Act) encourages states to develop and operate their own job safety and health plans. OSHA approves and monitors these plans. Twenty-four states, Puerto Rico and the Virgin Islands currently operate approved state plans: 22 cover both private and public (state and local government) employment; Connecticut, New Jersey, New York and the Virgin Islands cover the public sector only. States and territories with their own OSHA-approved occupational safety and health plans must adopt standards identical to, or at least as effective as, the Federal OSHA standards.

Consultation Services

Consultation assistance is available on request to employers who want help in establishing and maintaining a safe and healthful workplace. Largely funded by OSHA, the service is provided at no cost to the employer. Primarily developed for smaller employers with more hazardous operations, the consultation service is delivered by state governments employing professional safety and health consultants. Comprehensive assistance includes an appraisal of all mechanical systems, work practices, and occupational safety and health hazards of the workplace and all aspects of the employer's present job safety and health program. In addition, the service offers assistance to employers in developing and implementing an effective safety and health program. No penalties are proposed or citations issued for hazards identified by the consultant. OSHA provides consultation assistance to the employer with the assurance that his or her name and firm and any information about the workplace will not be routinely reported to OSHA enforcement staff.

Under the consultation program, certain exemplary employers may request participation in OSHA's Safety and Health Achievement Recognition Program (SHARP). Eligibility for participation in SHARP includes receiving a comprehensive consultation visit, demonstrating exemplary achievements in workplace safety and health by abating all identified hazards, and developing an excellent safety and health program.

Employers accepted into SHARP may receive an exemption from programmed inspections (not complaint or accident investigation inspections) for a period of 1 year. For more information concerning consultation assistance, see OSHA's website at www.osha.gov.

Voluntary Protection Programs (VPP)

Voluntary Protection Programs and on-site consultation services, when coupled with an effective enforcement program, expand employee protection to help meet the goals of the OSH Act. The VPPs motivate others to achieve excellent safety and health results in the same outstanding way as they establish a cooperative relationship between employers, employees, and OSHA.

For additional information on VPP and how to apply, contact the OSHA regional offices listed at the end of this publication.

Strategic Partnership Program

OSHA's Strategic Partnership Program, the newest member of OSHA's cooperative programs, helps encourage, assist, and recognize the efforts of partners to eliminate serious workplace hazards and achieve a high level of employee safety and health. Whereas OSHA's Consultation Program and VPP entail one-on-one relationships between OSHA and individual worksites, most strategic partnerships seek to have a broader impact by building cooperative relationships with groups of employers and employees. These partnerships are voluntary, cooperative relationships between OSHA, employers, employee representatives, and others (e.g., trade unions, trade and professional associations, universities, and other government agencies).

For more information on this and other cooperative programs, contact your nearest OSHA office, or visit OSHA's website at www.osha.gov.

Alliance Program

Through the Alliance Program, OSHA works with groups committed to safety and health, including businesses, trade or professional organizations, unions and educational institutions, to leverage resources and expertise to develop compliance assistance tools and resources and share information with employers and employees to help prevent injuries, illnesses and fatalities in the workplace.

Alliance Program agreements have been established with a wide variety of industries including meat, apparel, poultry, steel, plastics, maritime, printing, chemical, construction, paper and telecommunications. These agreements are addressing many safety and health hazards and at-risk audiences; including silica, fall protection, amputations, immigrant workers, youth and small businesses. By meeting the goals of the Alliance Program agreements (training and education, outreach and communication, and promoting the national dialogue on workplace safety and health), OSHA and the Alliance Program participants are developing and disseminating compliance assistance information and resources for employers and employees such as electronic assistance tools, fact sheets, toolbox talks, and training programs.

OSHA Training and Education

OSHA area offices offer a variety of information services, such as compliance assistance, technical advice, publications, audiovisual aids and speakers for special engagements. OSHA's Training Institute in Arlington Heights, IL, provides basic and advanced courses in safety and health for Federal and state compliance officers, state consultants, Federal agency personnel, and private sector employers, employees, and their representatives.

The OSHA Training Institute also has established OSHA Training Institute Education Centers to address the increased demand for its courses from the private sector and from other federal agencies. These centers are nonprofit colleges, universities, and other organizations that have been selected after a competition for participation in the program.

OSHA also provides funds to nonprofit organizations, through grants, to conduct workplace training and education in subjects where OSHA believes there is a lack of workplace training. Grants are awarded annually. Grant recipients are expected to contribute 20 percent of the total grant cost.

For more information on grants, training, and education, contact the OSHA Training Institute, Directorate of Training and Education, 2020 South Arlington Road, Arlington Heights, IL 60005, (847) 297-4810, or see *Outreach* on OSHA's website at www.osha.gov. For further information on any OSHA program, contact your nearest OSHA regional office listed at the end of this publication.

Information Available Electronically

OSHA has a variety of materials and tools available on its website at www.osha.gov. These include electronic compliance assistance tools, such as Safety and Health Topics, eTools, Expert Advisors; regulations, directives and publications; videos and other information for employers and employees. OSHA's software programs and compliance assistance tools walk you through challenging safety and health issues and common problems to find the best solutions for your workplace.

A wide variety of OSHA materials, including standards, interpretations, directives and more can be purchased on CD-ROM from the U.S. Government Printing Office, Superintendent of Documents, toll-free phone (866) 512-1800.

OSHA Publications

OSHA has an extensive publications program. For a listing of free or sales items, visit OSHA's website at www.osha.gov or contact the OSHA Publications Office, U.S. Department of Labor, 200 Constitution Avenue, NW, N-3101, Washington, DC 20210: Telephone (202) 693-1888 or fax to (202) 693-2498.

Contacting OSHA

To report an emergency, file a complaint, or seek OSHA advice, assistance, or products, call (800) 321-OSHA or contact your nearest OSHA Regional or Area office listed at the end of this publication. The teletypewriter (TTY) number is (877) 889-5627.

Written correspondence can be mailed to the nearest OSHA Regional or Area Office listed at the end of this publication or to OSHA's national office at: U.S. Department of Labor, Occupational Safety and Health Administration, 200 Constitution Avenue, N.W., Washington, DC 20210.

By visiting OSHA's website at www.osha.gov, you can also:

- file a complaint online,
- submit general inquiries about workplace safety and health electronically, and
- find more information about OSHA and occupational safety and health.

OSHA Regional Offices

Region I
(CT,* ME, MA, NH, RI, VT*)
JFK Federal Building, Room E340
Boston, MA 02203
(617) 565-9860

Region II
(NJ,* NY,* PR,* VI*)
201 Varick Street, Room 670
New York, NY 10014
(212) 337-2378

Region III
(DE, DC, MD,* PA, VA,* WV)
The Curtis Center
170 S. Independence Mall West
Suite 740 West
Philadelphia, PA 19106-3309
(215) 861-4900

Region IV
(AL, FL, GA, KY,* MS, NC,* SC,*
TN*)
61 Forsyth Street, SW, Room 6T50
Atlanta, GA 30303
(404) 562-2300

Region V
(IL, IN,* MI,* MN,* OH, WI)
230 South Dearborn Street
Room 3244
Chicago, IL 60604
(312) 353-2220

Region VI
(AR, LA, NM,* OK, TX)
525 Griffin Street, Room 602
Dallas, TX 75202
(972) 850-4145

Region VII
(IA,* KS, MO, NE)
Two Pershing Square
2300 Main Street, Suite 1010
Kansas City, MO 64108-2416
(816) 283-8745

Region VIII
(CO, MT, ND, SD, UT,* WY*)
1999 Broadway, Suite 1690
PO Box 46550
Denver, CO 80202-5716
(720) 264-6550

Region IX
(AZ,* CA,* HI,* NV,* and
American Samoa, Guam and
the Northern Mariana Islands)
90 7th Street, Suite 18-100
San Francisco, CA 94103
(415) 625-2547

Region X
(AK,* ID, OR,* WA*)
1111 Third Avenue, Suite 715
Seattle, WA 98101-3212
(206) 553-5930

* These states and territories operate their own OSHA-approved job safety and health programs and cover state and local government employees as well as private sector employees. The Connecticut, New Jersey, New York and Virgin Islands plans cover public employees only. States with approved programs must have standards that are identical to, or at least as effective as, the Federal OSHA standards.

Note: To get contact information for OSHA Area Offices, OSHA-approved State Plans and OSHA Consultation Projects, please visit us online at www.osha.gov or call us at 1-800-321-OSHA.